Foreword by Cardinal Se

Living
& Serving
in the Way of
St. Francis

Reflections from Franciscan Volunteers

Edited by Julie McElmurry

Living & Serving in the Way of St. Francis
Reflections from Franciscan Volunteers
Edited by Julie McElmurry

Cover Illustration: John Manders
Cover and book design: Tau Publishing Design Department

For information regarding permission, write to:
Tau Publishing, LLC
Attention: Permissions Dept.
4727 North 12th Street
Phoenix, AZ 85014

ISBN 978-1-61956-466-4

First Edition April 2015
10 9 8 7 6 5 4 3 2 1

Published and printed in the United States of America by Tau Publishing, LLC, an imprint of Vesuvius Press Incorporated.

♻ Text printed on 30% post-consumer waste recycled paper.

For additional inspirational books visit us at TauPublishing.com

TauPublishing.com

Words of Inspiration

Rough Days
Hot Sun
Long Bus rides
We are Challenged
Being misunderstood
Making mistakes
We are challenged
At the end of the day
We come together
Carrying our Crosses
We come together in prayer
To lighten our burden
We talk to God
We listen to God
We become one with him
He lightens our burden
He makes the very crosses we carry worth it
The smiles
The strangers we meet
The time for prayer
The beauty of life.

—Poem by Taylor A. Martin, FrancisCorps

Contents

Foreword

It is a great joy to mark the publishing of this book containing the reflections of young adult volunteers who have sought to live and serve in the spirit and path of Saint Francis of Assisi. These volunteers give the Church such hope and joy and demonstrate the vitality of Christian witness and service.

Our Catholic understanding of service flows from Holy Thursday when Jesus washed the feet of his Apostles and commanded them to do the same for others. The Holy Father, Pope Francis, followed this command by washing the feet of prisoners in a Roman prison, celebrating the Feast of the Lord's Supper, not in a church, but in that very prison. The Holy Father's actions challenge us to glimpse the truth and message of the Gospel. With a simple gesture, Pope Francis has tested our assumptions regarding power, authority and leadership. As he told the prisoners, this is a symbol, it is a sign. "Washing your feet means I am at your service," he said.

I pray that as you reflect upon your own call to service in light of Testament of Saint Francis that you will be moved to heed Pope Francis' call and become ministers capable of warming people's hearts; walking with them in the night, dialoguing with them about their hopes and desires; mending their brokenness; allowing them to help us in understanding our own brokenness; and bringing the joy of the Gospel to all we meet. Like Saint Francis may you preach the Gospel in all that you do - using words when necessary.

With all good wishes and assurance of a remembrance in my prayers, I am

Sincerely yours in Christ,

Cardinal Seán Patrick O'Malley, OFM Cap
Archbishop of Boston

Preface

A major characteristic of the writings of Francis of Assisi is that they were written after experience. They are the expression of a lived human experience. Written toward the end of his life, Francis' Testament is no exception to that. As he himself wrote, it is more than a testament. To use his own words, this writing of his is remembrance, admonition, exhortation, and testament altogether.

Francis of Assisi may not have gotten any high scholarly education, but he certainly had his way with words. Remembrance (in Latin *recordatio*) is more than bringing back to memory; it is a return to the core, to the heart. Admonition (in Latin *admonitio*) is deeper than a warning; it is a call to the mind, to thinking and reflecting. Exhortation (in Latin *exhortatio*) is more incitement than simple encouragement. And Testament (in Latin *testamentum*) should not be understood as a last will, but rather as a testimony, an evidence of truth.

Since he wrote it, Francis' Testament has inspired many men and women, and not only religious. Because that writing carries what made Francis alive, what made his life, it can speak to others and inspire them. It inspired me from the day I read it and continues to inspire my life. It inspired Julie McElmurry from the days that she was introduced to the writings of Francis. It inspired folks she has been working with.

May Francis' Testament inspire the readers of this book.

—Jean-François Godet-Calogeras
Saint Bonaventure University

Introduction

In his Testament, St. Francis of Assisi tells us that God led him to be among suffering people (the lepers) and that, over time, what had once been bitter to him became sweet. He lived among, befriended, and became as a brother to them. This change of heart happened because they welcomed him into their lives and loved him first. Thanks to the Franciscan Service Network, this experience of St. Francis is one which happens daily.

Franciscan Service Network programs invite men and women to follow in the poor and humble footprints of St. Francis just as he sought to follow in the poor and humble footprints of Jesus. Through Franciscan Service Network [www.franciscanservicenetwork. org] programs, people like you commit to serve in myriad ways for weeks, months, or years at a time. In this book, you will read stories from a Bolivian prison to a Philadelphia homeless shelter and everywhere in between. In each place, Franciscan volunteers become as brothers and sisters to people who are suffering.

The staff members of these Franciscan programs accomplished a remarkable task as they invited then-current volunteers and alumni to contribute to this project. This book could not have been written by one person as these stories — funny, sad, inspiring, challenging or unbelievable — have been lived by many people.

Provocative questions accompany each story and invite you to share your own. By reading and using the book regularly, volunteers have been given a useful tool for formation in the tradition of St. Francis of Assisi. Current volunteers will find in this book an invaluable tool as they reflect on their weeks, months or year of service. Alumni of year of service programs will recall their ministry and experiences. People considering volunteer service will read that each of us can perform extraordinary service when we volunteer as a community.

Thanks to Franciscan Scholar Professor Jean-François Godet-Calogeras, these stories connect profoundly to the Testament, which an ill St. Francis wrote, shortly before he died. Jean-François, an early and earnest supporter of this project, generously gave his permission to utilize and print here his, never-before-published, English language translation of the Testament of St. Francis of Assisi. The Testament is one way St. Francis continues to speak to us across these 800 years of history and another way we can get to know him and his intentions better. Jean-François gave a year's worth of guidance as this book was carried and cared for on its own pilgrimage to its final destination: your hands. Kaitlin Depuydt companioned me on this journey as well. Her wisdom and assurance illuminated the unknown path we followed to get this book to you.

Upon studying Jean-François' translation of the Testament, I discovered forty different themes which were assigned as writing prompts to collect stories and reflections of Franciscan Service Network volunteers and alumni. I create in-person and online presentations and retreats through Franciscan Passages [www.franciscanpassages.org]. Every talk I give has its foundation in the writings of St. Francis and St. Clare. They left us a treasure trove of poems, letters, testaments and other writings which paint a vivid picture of who they were and what they believed.

You will enjoy reading these stories. I hope that reading the Testament of St. Francis of Assisi and experiences of Franciscan volunteers will whet your appetite for discovering even more of his writings and encourage you to serve in the spirit of the Franciscan Service Network. May God's peace be with you.

—Julie McElmurry, M.S. M.A.
Director of Franciscan Passages
www.franciscanpassages.org
Charlotte, NC
Holy Week, 2015

How to Use This Book

The Testament of St. Francis of Assisi

He wrote this as he lay dying on his sick bed in order to clarify what he had been saying with his actions all along. Read the Testament at least once as you begin using this book. You will find that it always awaits your attention, revealing deeper, more poignant thoughts of St. Francis himself as you re-read it.

Reflections by Franciscan Service Volunteers

Franciscan volunteers wrote these reflections based on forty themes found in the Testament. Each took their time with the assigned theme, mulling it over and reaching back into the memory of their own weeks, months or years of Franciscan service to share these thought-provoking stories. They left their homes, their hometowns and their friends to go and be among suffering people, who welcomed them first.

Questions for Reflection

These provocative questions, which follow each reflection, invite you to share your own stories. These questions are most useful when shared with another. If you are a current Franciscan volunteer, use this within your community of volunteers. St. Francis' own experience will resonate with your own. His words are not just dusty souvenirs meant for climate-controlled library shelves, but speak to us with spirit and life, beckoning us from our comfort zones. Just as God inspired St. Francis to write these words 800 years ago, God can use them to inspire you, today.

Text of Testament of St. Francis of Assisi

---

[1]The Lord gave me, brother Francis, to begin to do penance in this way: While I was in sin, it seemed excessively bitter to me to see lepers. [2]And the Lord himself led me among them and I did mercy with them. [3]And when I left them that which seemed bitter to me had been changed into sweetness of the spirit and the body; and afterward I lingered a little and left the world [of Assisi].

[4]And the Lord gave me such faith in churches that I would simply pray and speak in this way: [5]"We adore you, Lord Jesus Christ, and to all your churches throughout the world, and we bless you, for through your holy cross you have redeemed the world."

[6]Afterward the Lord gave me and still gives me such faith in priests who live according to the form of the holy Roman Church because of their order, that if they were to persecute me, I would still have recourse to them. [7]And if I possessed as much wisdom as Solomon had and I came upon pitiful priests of this world, I would not preach contrary to their will in the parishes in which they live. [8]And I want to fear, love, and honor them and all others as my lords. [9]And I do not want to consider sin in them because I discern the Son of God in them and they are my lords. [10]And I do this because I see nothing corporally of the most high Son of God in this world except his most holy Body and most holy Blood which they receive and which they alone minister to others. [11]And these most holy mysteries I want to have honored above all things and to be venerated and to have them placed in precious places. [12]Wherever I come upon his most holy written words in unbecoming places, I want to collect them up and I ask that they be collected and placed in a suitable place. [13]And we should honor and venerate all theologians and those who minister the most holy divine words as those who minister to us spirit and life.

---

[14]*And after the Lord gave me brothers, no one showed me what I should do, but the Most High himself revealed to me that I should live according to the form of the Holy Gospel.* [15]*And I had it written down in a few words and simply and the Lord Pope confirmed it for me.* [16]*And those who came to receive that life gave everything which they might have to the poor;* [17]*and we were content with one tunic, patched inside and out, those who wanted, with a belt and breechers, and we did not want to have more.* [18]*We said the Office, the clerics according to the other clerics, the laics said the Our Father, and quite willingly we stayed in churches.* [19]*And we were without learning, and subject to all.* [20]*And I was working with my hands, and I want to work; and I firmly want all the other brothers to work in some work that is honest.* [21]*Those who do not know how to work shall learn, not out of any desire of receiving wages for their work, but to give example and to avoid idleness.* [22]*And when we are not paid for our work, let us have recourse to the table of the Lord, begging alms from door to door.* [23]*As salutation, the Lord revealed to me that we are to say: "The Lord give you peace!"*

[24]*The brothers shall beware that they by no means receive churches, poor dwellings and all the other things that are built for them, unless they were befitting the holy poverty which we have promised in the Rule, and they shall always be guests there like pilgrims and strangers.* [25]*And I firmly command all of the brothers through obedience that, wherever they are, they shall not dare to seek any letter from the Roman Curia either personally or through an intermediary, neither for a church or for another place or under the guise of preaching or even for the persecution of their bodies;* [26]*but wherever they have not been received, they shall flee into another land to do penance with the blessing of God.*

²⁷*And I firmly want to obey the minister general of this fraternity and another guardian whom it might please him to give me. ²⁸And I want to be so captive in his hands that I cannot go anywhere or do anything beyond obedience and his will, for he is my lord. ²⁹And although I may be simple and infirm, I want nonetheless always to have a cleric who will do the Office with me as it is contained in the Rule. ³⁰And all the other brothers shall be bound to obey their guardians and to do the Office according to the Rule. ³¹And those who would be found who do not do the Office according to the Rule and who want to alter it in any way or who are not Catholics, the brothers shall be bound through obedience that wherever they find such one they must bring him to the custodian who is nearest to that place where they have found him. ³²And the custodian shall be firmly bound through obedience to guard him strongly as a prisoner day and night, so that he cannot be snatched from his hands until he can personally bring him into the hands of his minister. ³³And the minister shall be firmly bound through obedience to send him with brothers who shall guard him as a prisoner day and night until they bring him before the Lord of Ostia who is the lord, protector, and corrector of the entire fraternity.*

³⁴*And the brothers shall not say: This is another Rule, because this is a remembrance, an admonition, an exhortation, and my testament, which I, little brother Francis, do for all of you, my blessed brothers, so that we may observe in a better catholic manner the Rule which we have promised to the Lord.* ³⁵*And the general minister and all other ministers and custodians shall be bound through obedience not to add to or subtract from these words.* ³⁶*And they shall always have this writing with them along with the Rule.* ³⁷*And in all the chapters which they hold, when they read the Rule, they shall also read these words.* ³⁸*And I through obedience firmly command all my brothers, cleric and lay, not to place glosses on the Rule or on these words, saying: They are to be understood in this way.* ³⁹*But as the Lord has given me to speak and to write the Rule and these words simply and purely, so shall you understand them simply and purely, without gloss, and observe them with holy activity until the end.*

⁴⁰*And whoever shall have observed these things, may he be filled in heaven with the blessing of the most high Father and on earth with the blessing of his beloved Son with the most Holy Spirit the Paraclete and with all the virtues of heaven and all the saints.* ⁴¹*And I, little brother Francis, your servant, inasmuch as I can, confirm for you this most holy blessing both within and without.*

—Shortly before October 3, 1226

The Lord gave me, brother Francis, to begin to do penance in this way: While I was in sin, it seemed excessively bitter to me to see lepers (…) And when I left them that which seemed bitter to me had been changed into sweetness of the spirit and the body.[1][3]

Bitter to Sweet
Ian Peoples, Franciscan Community Volunteer

It is a difficult thing to face our own mortality, especially when we face it by looking on the face of someone we love who is dying. In September I looked down at my grandfather connected to life support machines, his heart was failing after becoming ill with a debilitating stomach virus. I had not seen my Grandpa Peoples for six long years and had not so much as spoken to him in that time. After traveling from Minnesota to Altoona, Pennsylvania on a 30 hour trip via bus and train, I was now able to be with him in his last hours of life. It was a bitter feeling and I was deeply saddened, but I was also grateful to God in ways more than one.

I was grateful for the righteous and faithful life my Grandpa lived. He was a county judge for many years, and he had the respect of many colleagues and citizens; a testament to this was the visitation at the funeral home of a man who came to pay his last respects to my grandpa. My grandpa had sentenced the said man to juvenile detention center in days gone by, and this man was grateful for him having done so. Grandpa Peoples was a man of God. The Bishop of the Diocese of Altoona, a close friend of his, administered his last rites and also presided at his funeral Mass.

The Honorable Thomas G. Peoples Jr. knew of my gratitude to him because of the letter he received from me just a week before he became ill. Inspired by a longing to reconnect with my grandpa after years of not exchanging even a few words. I wrote him a letter; he was not one to speak on the phone. In it, I detailed my volunteer service with the Franciscan Sisters of Little Falls, Minnesota. More importantly, I related to him the love and gratitude I have for my family, and for the man that he had raised my father to be. It was important to me that my grandpa know the love his son, my father, has shown to his children, and this is what I explained in the letter.

Without my knowing it, God allowed me to say goodbye to my grandpa. I was afforded the privilege of thanking him, a man I still feel like I hardly know. One thing I am assured of though, my grandpa now rests in His Glory. I hope to see him again one fateful day, until then I hope to enjoy all the blessed flavors and fruits of this gift of life, bitter and sweet alike.

Questions for Reflection

St. Francis was led to be among people who once disgusted him. He, like everyone else in his day, avoided them at all costs until God led him to be among them. Eventually, he came to know and love them as he cared for them. Describe a time when something turned from bitter to sweet in your own life.

Describe a time when God led you to be among a group of people who needed you.

²And the Lord himself led me among them and I did mercy with them.

Apprehension to Action
Hannah Pinter, Franciscan Outreach Volunteers

For my service year, I am a night-shift supervisor for a women's dorm at a homeless shelter. I'm a quiet-natured person to begin with, so trying to respond to the needs, complaints, and conflicts of 40 women, many of whom could be my mother, has been significantly challenging at times. Even after 8 months here, I still struggle with fear and anxiety because I never know what to expect when I arrive at work. Every night is different.

As I have dealt with this throughout the year, God has continually reminded me that I am not alone in my position. It's amazing to remember that He is God, and He is always with us and to meditate on what that means. More than that, God has shown me how much support I received from the women I am serving. When I can't respond to everyone's requests at once or give everyone the listening ear or advice they need, I see the women stepping in and helping each other. Many of them also take a moment to offer an encouraging word to me when they see that I am busy or stressed. It's been a gift to find community in this way at the shelter and to realize how much God reaches us and sustains us through others.

Questions for Reflection

St. Francis recognized that it was God who led him to be among lepers, who were the most reviled and outcast of his society. Think back to a time when you were new to a place. What fears did you have in the beginning?

How has God reached or sustained you through other people?

Be Here, Now
Kristine Origone, Franciscan Community Volunteers

When I joined the Franciscan Community Volunteers, I desired to surrender fully to God. Initially, this felt like a betrayal to my home community. So, while I desired to give 100%, I was offering 10, maybe 15%. Through this intimate community, I could see my naïveté. Truth is, intimacy deepens when we are accepted and loved through our vulnerability and insecurities.

Opportunity for intimacy presented itself early on through a courageous member's letter. Some in our community rejected it, and him for writing it, while others embraced it, and were thereafter transformed. For the first time, I saw somebody who cared enough to speak out. He shared his frustrations and challenged us who were settling for partial engagement. In that, I saw something real, something that I was called to, and something I was so afraid of. However, I recognized a sense of freedom and truth in that. I was challenged to experience hurt and rejection and knew that some people in this community wouldn't like me. Some people in life won't accept me, but that is all I have to offer. As the saints say, we are called to be faithful, not perfect. So despite my flaws, my brokenness, and my insecurities, I actively pursued a complete offering of myself.

Questions for Reflection

St. Francis had a lot to leave behind when he chose to leave his status, comfort, and wealth in Assisi to follow the unknown path where God beckoned. As you've transitioned in your life, how have you kept connected with people in your old place while forging new relationships and connecting with people in your new place?

What holds you back from fully immersing yourself in your here and now?

⁴And the Lord gave me such faith in churches that I would simply pray and speak in this way: ⁵"We adore you, Lord Jesus Christ, and to all your churches throughout the world, and we bless you, for through your holy cross you have redeemed the world."

Church
Jeff Sved, Franciscan Mission Service & Franciscan Volunteer Ministry

Carpentry workshop, visitor meeting space, fútbol field, court room, dining room, chapel.

The central courtyard in El Centro de Reinserción Social in Quillacollo, Bolivia fills all these roles during a typical week for the inmates there. Almost every prison in Bolivia is built around that multi-use central space. It is where we talk, where we work, where we play, where we laugh, where we celebrate, and where we worship.

For "El Día de Los Presos," which is celebrated on the feast day of Mary of Mercy, there was a day-long celebration in this space that began with Mass and continued with lunch, dancing, dinner, and more dancing. I was blessed with the opportunity to participate in this day of community, sharing in the Eucharist and much more.

This coming together is what I think of as "church": a community that is defined not by their space, but how they use it. It is a beautiful community that shares life together, in the Mass and every other aspect of their lives.

Questions for Reflection

Have you found community in an unexpected place, like the writer did in a Bolivian prison?

In what way can your Church building be used to help people share life together or serve others' need?

⁴And the Lord gave me such faith in churches that I would simply pray and speak in this way: ⁵"We adore you, Lord Jesus Christ, and to all your churches throughout the world, and we bless you, for through your holy cross you have redeemed the world."

Inviting Others to the Church
Stephen F. Scott, Franciscan Mission Service

During the Bolivian festival of Santa Vera Cruz, I saw how the church was home, not just for those attending, but for the whole community. Before walking into the church itself, I saw people from various Bolivian cultures come to pray at this site which had been considered holy since before the Spanish had arrived. So many people were gathered outside praying earnestly for help that it felt strange and a bit intimidating for me to walk past them to enter the church, a building that did not have doors, but a simple opening on one side.

However, upon entering the church, I found a vibrant and welcoming community of prayer. Many of the people I saw from outside had also entered and joined the community there for prayer. Many people would not stay the entire time, but their presence awakened in me the realization of how our churches are for everyone. Together we build up not only our church buildings, but also God's Kingdom, just at St. Francis did during his life. Although I entered the church with some fear, I found myself being sent to open the entrance more, inviting others to the Church.

Questions for Reflection

Francis says that we should adore Christ in churches throughout the world. Describe some churches you have visited.

In what way can you, like the writer, invite others to the Church?

⁶Afterward the Lord gave me and still gives me such faith in priests who live according to the form of the holy Roman Church because of their order, that if they were to persecute me, I would still have recourse to them.

Faith in Priests
Meg Masciola, Cap Corps – East

During my volunteer year, I struggled with community prayer. It was difficult to adjust to having so many other people around all the time when I wanted to talk to God! During the week, I prayed in the mornings and evenings with my roommates, I went to Mass with my students, and even on the weekends we were always going to Mass or evening prayer together. Frustrated, one Sunday I went to Mass alone. In his homily, the priest said, "We are not meant to do anything alone." I smiled. God speaks to each individual heart through His priests, no matter how many people are sitting in the pews. Soon after I began to listen during community prayer. I learned I could hear God's message through the priests, Capuchin brothers and my fellow volunteers. Although I still needed some time for my personal spiritual life, I began to trust that I would hear God's voice clearly when He spoke through others in my community.

Questions for Reflection

Describe a time when God has spoken to you through His priests.

How do you find a balance between personal prayer and communal prayer?

⁷And if I possessed as much wisdom as Solomon had and I came upon pitiful priests of this world, I would not preach contrary to their will in the parishes in which they live.

Leading with Humility
Sarah Hoffeditz, Franciscan Mission Service

A few months after I began my volunteer term, there arose a need for me to become the temporary house manager of our guest house, which also hosted our intentional community. One month became two, then eventually five months before a new house manager was found. It was difficult to balance being an equal member of our community with being the person who was ultimately in charge of our house, including the chore schedule. I never got it perfectly right, but I started to realize that having authority doesn't have to elevate you. If you are fair, seek others' opinions, and always try to do things with the blessing of the group, then it becomes possible to remain a relatively equal member of the community.

Questions for Reflection

Describe a time you have been in authority. How did you interact with others?

In the spirit of St. Francis, humility is an important leadership quality. How can you serve as a leader with humility?

⁹And I do not want to consider sin in them because I discern the Son of God in them and they are my lords.

Growing through Relationships
Laura Castro, Cap Corps – Midwest

When I was serving with my volunteer program, another foreign volunteer arrived with great expectations for the work she would be able to do. She had many talents and a playful spirit. However, she clashed with the culture of the local community, and she wasn't the most collaborative housemate when it came to chores.

At first, I struggled greatly with her behavior and felt personally attacked by her indifference to helping out around the house and her lack of respect for the work culture. This affected my friendship with her and led me to avoid interactions with her. I didn't want to focus on Christ in her work; I only saw the things that made me angry. Through prayer and conversations with my intentional community, I was able to identify my real issues with her. I realized that she reminded me of the things I didn't like in myself: stubbornness; disobedience; impatience.

I accepted the realization that we are all on different paths when it comes to our relationship with God and how we live life to reflect that relationship. My housemate had her own lessons to learn, and I couldn't expedite that process. I could only grow in loving unconditionally and accepting her as God accepts me.

Questions for Reflection

How do you see the presence of Christ in someone you have a hard time with?

Describe a time when working with a difficult person that helped you better understand yourself.

[10] And I do this because I see nothing corporally of the most high Son of God in this world except his most holy Body and most holy Blood which they receive and which they alone minister to others.

Thinking about Eucharist
Kristen Zielinski-Nalen, Franciscan Mission Service

Padre Teo held up the Eucharist in front of all the children who were sitting on their little cafeteria stools, surrounding the makeshift Sunday altar on three sides. They sang, "El vive, el vive, el vive, vive. Vive Jesús, el Señor." (He lives. He lives. He lives. Jesus the Lord lives.) The orphans and street children shouted the proclamation of faith earnestly.

Anytime I joined them for Sunday Mass, I wept while they sang. I, while blessed with all that life could offer in physical comfort, education and family support, doubted the real presence of Jesus Christ in the Eucharist. I, formed and versed in all things Catholic, sent as a missionary, bearing the light of the Gospel in places of darkness, was a phony.

Meanwhile, "the least of these" who had been abandoned by family, whose self-esteem was ground into the dirt, whose earthly possessions were two t-shirts, one pair of flip flops and mended sweatpants, proclaimed with all his might in a chorus of compañeros that Yes! Jesus is the Lord, alive in the Eucharist.

Help me, Lord, to believe as these little ones believe, to trust in You as they trust.

Questions for Reflection

When have you seen the wealth of the "least of these" and the poverty of those who have "all that life could offer?"

Describe an experience you've had in thinking about, receiving, or distributing the Eucharist.

[11]And these most holy mysteries I want to have honored above all things and to be venerated and to have them placed in precious places.

Precious Places
Laura Kolar, Cap Corps – Midwest

The chapel reminded me of a cave — stone and wood and earth married in a quiet, expansive space. By the altar, there is a wooden statue of the risen Lord emerging from stone slabs. Early on the morning of Holy Saturday, the chapel was dim, filled with shadowy corners, and a small assembly of friars and volunteers gathered off on one side to pray Morning Prayer. My part was chanting Psalm 88. I stood up at the lectern and found myself face to face with a small window I hadn't previously noticed. Entranced by the light that beckoned from the window, I was filled with a hushed hopefulness there in the darkness. As I sang to the light, I poured out the words of the anguished psalmist: "All day I call on you, Lord; I stretch out my hands to you." I felt as though I was crying out my own darkness and every story of suffering of the people I lived with and served with. It was that moment for me, in that cavernous, reverent space, that the "holy mysteries" — the pain, betrayal, sacrifice, longing, hope, love, and joy, all wrapped up in Christ's Passion and Resurrection — met the world of South Chicago, in all the rawness and drama of the human experience. This, I felt in my soul, was the point of it all — Christ dying to reach into our darkness.

Questions for Reflection

Describe a meaningful experience you have had in an actual space of a church or chapel.

When have you been filled with a "hushed hopefulness" in a time of darkness?

[12]Wherever I come upon his most holy written words in unbecoming places, I want to collect them up and I ask that they be collected and placed in a suitable place.

Suitable Places
Alana Small, Change a Heart Franciscan Volunteer Program

It feels odd to say that the car was a sacred space for me during my year of service. Usually the spaces I choose are outdoors, or rooms that I have taken the time to arrange in ways that help me be still and listen. In this case, I had a one hour commute between home and my service site, which limited opportunities to find quiet spaces indoors or out.

I had the choice of waiting until there was time to find a more convenient space or choosing to let the present space be enough. I chose the present space. Choosing the present space, meant choosing to ride in silence or listen to music that helped me relax and reflect. These were the ways that I kept my sacred space clean and tidy, free from emotional or mental distractions.

God met me in an inconvenient space that year. He also met me in the "inconvenient" times when my clients or community needed me. I like to think that I learned something that year through the challenge of acknowledging and accepting sacredness as it was given, not as I thought it should appear.

Questions for Reflection

St. Francis revered the word of God and the name of God. It is said that even seeing a few branches crisscrossed in the shape of a cross would cause him to praise God. In the course of a typical day, when can you carve out times to pray and reflect?

Of all the "unbecoming places" you have visited in your life, describe one where you felt close to God.

[13]And we should honor and venerate all theologians and those who minister the most holy divine words as those who minister to us spirit and life.

Those who Minister
Meghan Monahan, Change a Heart Franciscan Volunteer Program

When I entered my year of service, I felt very comfortable talking about my faith with others. But I quickly realized that my comfort ended when the conversation became anything more than an academic discussion. My community member Brenda, on the other hand, prayed fluidly out loud and spoke directly to God like a dear friend. Her courage to be raw and vulnerable in prayer inspired me to open up a more authentic relationship with the Lord. I expressed to Brenda that an intimacy with God had always been my greatest desire, and her example helped me finally let my walls down. Throughout the year, we began to pray together often. I felt at peace in her presence, not ashamed to speak what was on my heart. To show my appreciation for Brenda, I try to let her know how my faith is still deepening. She smiles widely when I tell her about the days that I feel particularly close to God or when she hears me raise my voice in song.

Questions for Reflection

St. Francis encourages others to be grateful for the theologians and all those who minister to us. Name some of the people who have ministered to your "spirit and life." What can you do to express your gratitude to them this week?

What would it take for you to be more "raw and vulnerable" in your prayer life?

14...No one showed me what I should do

Ministry of Presence
Annemarie Barrett, Franciscan Mission Service

While sharing life with Cochabambinos in Bolivia, I am challenged every day to surrender to being led by the spirit of God. I rarely have the certainty of knowing what to do next. I am constantly invited into humility and minority, growing in our Franciscan charism by learning to receive hospitality just as generously as it is being offered to me.

One day in my ministry, we had just finished a meeting with Doña Nelly and she invited me to join her for lunch in her home. I was a bit anxious, as I usually am, about being a burden. We finished the meal and I had no idea what to do next. Should I leave? Should I stay? I decided to follow Doña Nelly's lead. We started talking and soon we were weaving bracelets together. Her sister joined us and we shared the afternoon together, talking about their families, their culture, their struggles and their joys. We grew as a community. By following her lead, I believe I was listening to the spirit of God, I was being invited beyond what I knew into a humble ministry of presence.

Questions for Reflection

Describe a time when you were glad you accepted the hospitality of others.

In times of uncertainty, how do you find the courage to trust what is next?

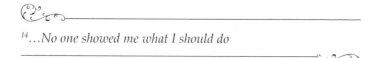
The Most Difficult to Love
Sean Cooksey, Change a Heart Franciscan Volunteer Program

At Palm Sunday Mass during my senior year of college at my campus's chapel, before reading the gospel the presiding priest told all of us in attendance to slow ourselves down and let God put us into the story of Christ's passion. The results of this for me were astonishing. That morning I was put into the role of Judas Iscariot, Jesus' betrayer. This was something that I would have never expected. I felt the agony of his remorse for his betrayal after Jesus' death, and I suffered with him in the moments before his suicide. I was brought to tears and was overcome with these emotions. Judas is arguably the most hated character in the bible, and I genuinely felt sorry for him. I was asking myself, "What can this possibly mean?"

During my time as a volunteer, the meaning of this vision was revealed to me. I was shadowing one of my coworkers who was leading a seminar for people who were looking for more stable housing. One of the men who was at the seminar told about his current living situation, in which he was being blatantly taken advantage of by his landlord. He was having a lot of trouble finding a better situation for himself. I also learned that he was a convicted sex offender, guilty of child molestation, and out of prison for almost twenty years. Much to my surprise, I was overwhelmed with compassion for this man. I felt sorrow for his helplessness in his situation, and I was angered by injustices being done to him. Sex offenders are among the most despised people in our society, and

I was empathizing with one who was right in front of me. Again I asked myself, "What can this possibly mean?"

Later on that day, while I was in private reflection, I finally made the connection between these two stories. During that Mass on Palm Sunday God was showing me how to love others the way he loves them, even the ones who are most difficult to love. God was also showing me that nobody is beyond the reach of his mercy. Today this reminds me of how Saint Francis was moved to compassion for the lepers outside of Assisi and began ministering to them. I imagine that this compassion scared Francis as it scared me. Love of that kind is very countercultural. Now I can only pray that this stays with me as it did for Francis.

Questions for Reflection

St. Francis makes it clear that the path he followed was one chosen by God and revealed to him only step by step. Never did Francis have the luxury of the big picture. As you discern your own path, step by step, how do you react when there are unexpected twists and turns along the way?

Describe a time when you were shocked by someone's life story. How did you respond at the time? How would you respond now?

Each Other's Joys
Martha Ligas, Change a Heart Franciscan Volunteer Program

I'd heard it time and time again that it is in giving that we receive, but it wasn't until I was called into my volunteer community of 11 young people that I truly experienced the meaning of this paradox. What moves my heart most about my community is that the call to serve one another seems to come naturally, reminding me that we really are created to love. Sometimes I just can't help myself from standing back in awe of the selflessness of my community. Like earlier this year when Chris had a day off, yet chose to spend the day preparing a feast for us when we came home. Or when a group of us walked home in the rain one night, tired and soaked, and we were greeted by the rest with dry clothes and hearty bowls of soup. As a community we also come together to dance in each other's joys and cry in each other's sorrows, like when we all stopped what we were doing to celebrate when Joy learned she got accepted to medical school, and all paused to give hugs and a sympathy card when Kim's dog passed away. Although I spend my days serving at a non-profit, it is through the love that my community shares that I have truly learned what it means to give of yourself.

Questions for Reflection

Francis says the Lord gave him brothers. Who are some of the brothers and sisters the Lord has given to you?

The "hearty bowl of soup" in this author's story can be a metaphor for lots of things. When has someone "met you at the door" with a hearty bowl of soup when you needed it most?

Living in Community
Zach Buchel, Franciscan Outreach Volunteers

"You're the average of the five people you spend the most time with." is a quote by Jim Rohn.

If this quote has any truth to it, I am an incredibly lucky man. Living in community, we have picked up on each other's "ism's" as Gracie calls them. These "ism's" are the quirks that are uniquely a part of us. For instance, I say "phenomenal" more often than others. Sara's enthusiasm for any idea is demonstrated by the phrase, "OH MY GOSH, CAN WE PLEASE DO THAT!" Whenever I have to ask for a second opinion about the seasoning in a meal we're serving, Mike is there to say, "Why not? You ain't driving!" This is just the kind of motivation I need to get a dish completed. These instances demonstrate the beauty of living in community. We become the average of each other. Not only have I gained a vastly more encompassing perspective of the world from living with these folks, I have also picked up on each of their strengths. I am eternally grateful that God has deemed me worthy to receive such an abundance of good personalities into my life. If this community happens to be the cards God has dealt for me, I have been dealt a royal flush.

Questions for Reflection

Just as the Lord provided St. Francis with companions, you find yourself surrounded by companions at times. Name the five people you spend the majority of your time with. In what ways have they influenced you?

Think about some of the people you've encountered recently who have changed your perspective on the world.

[15]I had it written down in a few words and simply...

A Few Simple Words
Brian Niemiec, Cap Corps, New York

Few and simple words are not my strong suit, but every once in a while God continues to show me that he speaks not through words, but through actions and quiet. During my year of service I worked at a retreat center in Garrison, New York. One retreat was with a high school senior class from New York City. Talks and group discussions on vocation, future goals, and God's presence in the journey resonated well with previous groups. It was not what these students wanted to hear.

We started to panic! How were we going to tell them that God was with them through the changes in their lives? How will they know he is there to help? Well, then we got to the activities: team building games, group projects, and communal prayer; and the result was miraculous. The students were bonding with each other, and they were trusting each other, and you could see the weight on their shoulders lessen. God was there with them, and they felt and knew it! I didn't have to explain it to them.

Sometimes words are overrated.

Questions for Reflection

What is something you need to say to someone in your life right now "in a few words and simply?"

Describe a time when you started to panic, but later the results were miraculous.

[16]And those who came to receive that life gave everything which they might have to the poor.

The Simple Approach
Tom Firme, Franciscan Volunteer Ministry

While hanging out with my friends in my hometown a few months ago, we walked around the grocery store and my friend bought a couple of new action figures for his girlfriend's son, he talked about how he needed to get the boy all of the newest toys and the amount of stress he heaped on himself in trying to be the boy's father figure.

At that moment, I realized the chasm between my attitude towards material goods and those held by my friends. Partly, my parents had conditioned me to break down brand identity and not put stock in goods. We never had money for new things anyway.

During my Franciscan Volunteer Ministry year, I gained a deep appreciation for the simple approach. I arrived with a modest amount of clothing — no dress clothes — along with my tuba, laptop and a couple other times. Notably, I decided I should leave my iPod behind.

My housemates and I decided not to have a television in the house. We needed each other and our St. Anthony of Padua community more than a glowing box.

Through Franciscan spirituality and time spent with people of the church and neighborhood, I learned more about detaching oneself from the stuff that fills our spaces, and incidentally, our lives.

Being one who would constantly have music playing, I learned the value of Franciscan silence. I discovered that I didn't need background sounds while enjoying company.

These values have helped me recognize the urgency of presence to others that overrides desire for material goods. Once, my phone battery died during an evening I spent with a friend I hadn't seen in a few years. Losing access to the notifications and apps on my phone for a few hours was no matter since attention was of greater necessity.

Questions for Reflection

St. Francis' embrace of simple living is something which has inspired thousands of people to follow his example. How has your attitude toward material things evolved over the years?

What does living simply look like for you?

This author mentions limiting distractions in order to concentrate on conversations. How might you limit the distractions in your life?

[17]And we were content with one tunic, patched inside and out, those who wanted, with a belt and breechers, and we did not want to have more.

Material Possessions
Chris Calderone, Franciscan Volunteer Ministry

"Simple living. Surely, this includes living without many — if any — material possessions," I thought to myself as I packed an attic and a closet full of my belongings days before leaving for my year with Franciscan Volunteer Ministry. As I began packing musical instruments away, my eyes came to rest on my trumpet. "Maybe some of the kids at St. Anthony of Padua School would want to learn to play trumpet...maybe I should bring it." This thought process repeated itself with countless items that might "help" me serve others. Sure enough, I showed up in Camden, NJ with many more boxes than I had planned. I already felt a bit removed from the Gospel verses which inspired the Rule of St. Francis; I had certainly not sold my possessions, I had taken plenty more than a knapsack and shoes with me, and I only had room in the trunk for a small desktop crucifix.

During my year of service, I did use a fair amount of my personal resources and possessions to teach the students at St. Anthony's and to serve in other ways around the parish. At the same time, I also learned that some of the greatest acts of service need no help from material possessions. God blesses all of us with materials and resources, which can be used selfishly or selflessly. However, the greatest gifts we have from God are a ready heart, a willing spirit, and open hands. In the end, these gifts got me further in ministry than anything else I had brought with me. If we serve others with these gifts alone, God will provide the rest.

As for the trumpet, I left it home…the kids loved singing much more.

Questions for Reflection

Think about the resources and materials you own. Which do you use selfishly? Which do you use selflessly?

¹⁸We said the Office, the clerics according to the other clerics, the laics said the Our Father, and quite willingly we stayed in churches.

Gathering as Community
Mike Callahan, Franciscan Outreach Volunteers

In John's Gospel, Lazarus, "tied hand and foot with burial bands," had been dead for four days when he emerged from his tomb in response to Christ's call. Christ then commands those present, "Untie him, and let him go." (John 11:44, NAB)

There are times when God puts others in our lives to help remove the binding that we are unable to remove ourselves. The opportunity for this "untying" is ever-present within community life. Perhaps you entered your year of service with preconceived notions as to the causes of homelessness. Perhaps you struggle with the demands of working for social justice. Maybe you're unable to find common ground with someone from a different faith-tradition than your own, and instead choose to focus on the differences that separate you. Consider taking these bindings, with help from your community, to the Lord in prayer.

Everyone who accepts the challenge of living in community is asked to actively participate in the growth and betterment of those with whom they live and serve. Encourage this growth by gathering as a community to enter into dialogue with our Lord. As Paul relates in Romans 8:26, the Spirit can aid you in your weakness by interceding on your behalf in the form of words prayed aloud by another member of your community. Invite our Lord to command those around you to help untie the burial bands that may be keeping you from a more intimate relationship with Christ.

Questions for Reflection

The literate brothers were to pray the daily Office while the illiterate brothers were to pray the Our Father repeatedly throughout the day. In this way, friars prayed together although the words they used were not the same. How do you find common ground with those who come from a different faith tradition from yours?

In general, how can you be hospitable and warm by accommodating people who don't know what you know?

[19] And we were without learning, and subject to all.

My Favorite Prayer
Taylor A. Martin, FrancisCorps

Nightly prayer with my community started off as a program requirement. However, this part of my schedule quickly evolved into a life-giving experience, energizing me to take on the next day. One of my favorite prayers happens to be one of the simplest, Where did you see God today? I remember one night specifically, I was feeling rather passive, thinking that nothing really exciting happened, it was just another day. After hearing the question, I initially found myself wondering if I had seen God at all that day. After a couple of minutes in silent reflection, I found myself going over all the faces of the people I had interacted with. I was surprised when I realized I had actually seen so many smiles and acts of love. As my community members began to share their God moments, I felt inspired and reenergized because God had been present. In fact, I was even seeing God in my community members as they spoke. God had been present so many times during my day; I simply had not been open to seeing him.

Questions for Reflection

St. Francis, speaking out of humility as always, describes himself and the early brothers as being "without learning" and existing to serve others. As you think about your own call to serve others, what energizes you to do that?

In what simple, unsophisticated ways have you noticed God's presence in your life lately?

[20]And I was working with my hands, and I want to work; and I firmly want all the other brothers to work in some work that is honest.

Heart Pats
Maureen Burke, Cap Corps – East

While working with the homeless, I quickly learned that there is no magic wand to solve the world's problems of homelessness, underemployment, education, mental health, or burned bridges. No, we cannot always fix what lies before us. We cannot do everything, but we can do something. And we can do that something, enthusiastically, with our whole heart. At my agency, we celebrated big accomplishments and little breakthroughs just the same. When we felt our hearts overflowing because of the strength, resilience and courage we found in the work of our clients, we would bring our hand to our chest and call that moment a "heart pat." Whether I was writing out a clothing referral for the hundredth time, listening to a man talk about his rock collection, handing out toiletries, testifying in front of the city council, or advocating for more affordable housing, I would rejoice in the task before me and hold on to those heart pats. It may be true that we will not see the fruits of our labor and tasks will be incomplete, but a healthy dose of humility helps us realize that we cannot save the world on our own. We need each other, and we need God's grace to help us realize that we are not walking in circles. With each heart pat, we are guiding each other on a path home.

Questions for Reflection

St. Francis wanted his followers to work first and beg when the work was not enough to put food on the table for that day. In his Testament, he refers to it as work done with his hands. What kind of work with your hands are you called to do?

This author describes a "heart pat" as a gesture which indicates one's heart is overflowing because of the strength, resilience and courage around them. Describe a "heart pat" experience you have had recently.

²¹Those who do not know how to work shall learn, not out of any desire of receiving wages for their work, but to give example and to avoid idleness.

All I must Accomplish
Lianna Mueller, Cap Corps – East

While driving Hamidi to his doctor's appointment, we chat in the car on the way back to his home. Though I am listening to him, my mind is also thinking of all that I must accomplish. Back at the office, paperwork and forms to fill out are piled on the desk. There are phone calls to be made, emails to send, case notes to document.

When I arrive at his family's home, he invites me in. For a moment I hesitate, but know it would be hurtful to refuse. Hamidi's wife and daughters work to create a traditional African dish of fish, rice and vegetables, and the whole family and I sit around the large platter and visit. The family joyfully shares all they have with me, until I feel ready to burst.

Though a mound of work awaits me at the office, this moment of seeming idleness is the greatest work I am called to. Francis encouraged his brothers to work, yet he also knew that seeing Jesus Christ in the face of each and every person was the most important work. At times, Christ beckons us to step away from our "work" and allow ourselves to love and be loved in that moment.

Questions for Reflection

A "ministry of presence" is a way of being with people that may look like idleness from the outside, but it can be a time of relationship-building. Who needs this ministry of presence from you?

When has someone welcomed you into their home? What did that gesture mean?

22 And when we are not paid for our work, let us have recourse to the table of the Lord, begging alms from door to door.

Feeling of Total Helplessness
Benjamin Neville, Cap Corps – Midwest

Christmas day was getting closer as the days were growing shorter. My wife and I would try to willfully ignore the subject, but Christmas was coming. The subject of income loomed over us. Our parents and siblings would understand our financial constraints, but the disappointment of our nephews, particularly our godson, would be difficult to overcome. I was ashamed that we could barely afford the gas money home let alone a couple of simple gifts.

Privilege in life sheltered me from the feeling of total helplessness and shame associated with it. I had always been protected from saying, "I need help."

Even though seeking help was my only option, it took me days to ask my boss for it. He was running a donation-based Christmas store and had a few items left over. From the moment I finally asked for help to the moment I put those gifts in my car was one of the most powerful, transformative moments of my life. I seldom cry, but a mixture of joy and pain spurred the tears to trickle down my face. The joy of the overwhelming amount of love present in this world was juxtaposed against the pain of realizing how often many people experience this same helplessness.

Moving forward, how can I be more empathic and compassionate when offering help to others?

Questions for Reflection

St. Francis indicates that he wants his brothers to beg (that is what is meant by having recourse to the table of the Lord) for food when the work they did that day was not enough to cover their food. Sometimes, we find ourselves having to beg for food, money or attention. Sometimes, this is in a very palatable, formal way, but it is still begging. Think about some people who are modern day beggars. How do they go about their begging?

Maybe you are not used to asking people for help. How might you ask people for help when you need it?

²³*As salutation, the Lord revealed to me that we are to say: "The Lord give you peace!"*

Peace is not a Fuzzy Feeling
Diana Yaeger, Change a Heart Franciscan Volunteer Program

The red light blinked on the phone again. This had become a routine; another house had burnt down. I started with the preliminary paperwork as the fire department rattled off the address and number of people in the household. Then I reached the box I almost never had to check: casualties. This time we were going to meet a woman who had just lost her daughter.

We arrived on scene. There was no need to even enter the house; it was destroyed. Then we walked to the neighbor's house for what was sure to be a solemn meeting. In the cozy living room with concerned friends making calls to insurance companies, I sat with an elderly lady firmly holding my hand. In a thick European accent, Helga acknowledged her sadness but spoke of what God had done for her. "God has given us so much. My daughter, she was joy. She was loving and kind and a gift. A lot has happened to us. I lost my husband; and my daughter, she had a stroke. That is why she couldn't get out of the house. But God will never leave us." This is the truth.

Oh, how it looks as though death wins. We all meet our graves, whether death is unexpected or life is fading away. However, Jesus will not leave us. He looked weak, dying there on the cross but the grave could not hold the Son of God. When He is with us, we too have victory although we may look lost. This is the Lord's peace, which the world cannot give. The Lord's peace is not a fuzzy feeling, but peace with the Father. In Christ we are forgiven and no longer enemies of God.

St Francis used the greeting, "May the Lord give you peace," while begging for alms. We are all beggars before God. He created us, and now gives us peace in His Son. God will never leave us, but rather resurrect us from the grave. I was reminded of my peace that day when the red light blinked with the bad news. Death, where is your sting? Helga has peace, because she has Jesus.

Questions for Reflection

Some people bring a greeting of peace as part of their very presence. This author describes Helga as someone with an abiding peace. Describe someone you have met who, like Helga, possesses that. What have you learned from that person?

In this story, Helga describes her daughter as being the epitome of joy. In what ways do you bring joy and peace to people you meet, either with your very presence or with an actual greeting?

Frantic Stranger
Julio Guerrero, Cap Corps – Midwest

One day, a woman came into the literacy center. She seemed very frantic and asked me to help her use the computer. As I was helping her, I had to inquire about what she needed help with. She needed help using Google Maps. She volunteered the information that she was trying to find the name and address of a man that her son had accused of sexually abusing him.

Initially, I was frustrated that this woman would come to the literacy center asking for help with such a traumatic issue. Our job is to teach English — none of us are trained social workers. I asked myself: Why didn't she go to the police? Was she undocumented? Did she not feel that she could trust the police because of some prior experience? I encouraged her to take the name and address of this accused abuser to the police and file a report.

The twenty minutes I spent helping her flew by quickly. In the end, I don't know that I helped her in any tangible way; I only know that for some reason, the people she felt she could trust were the staff at a neighborhood literacy center. I can only hope that she and her family have found a way to work through this trauma, and that they have found some resolution.

In hindsight, I wonder: Could I have been a greater help to this woman had I spent more time focused on her dilemma than focusing on my discomfort because of it?

Questions for Reflection

Take a moment to put yourself in the writer's shoes. What more could you do for this woman who came into the literacy center?

When have you been the pilgrim or stranger? What hospitality was shown to you at that time?

24The brothers shall beware that they by no means receive churches, poor dwellings and all the other things that are built for them, unless they were befitting the holy poverty which we have promised in the Rule...

Wealth and Poverty
Augie Lindmark, Franciscan Community Volunteers

My service site was a mobile home park where the windows were rarely clean and the cracked sidewalk made you think yesterday's earthquake did some real damage. The truth is that Minnesota doesn't have many earthquakes, but we do have inequity.

Ten minutes was all it took for me to drive from a polished, central Minnesotan downtown to an aging mobile home community hidden from society's eye. The realities of the marginalized are uncovered in this juxtaposition of wealth and poverty. I learned that the inequities found in our communities (including socio-economic gaps) contain both promise and peril: promise because we have the potential to alleviate economic injustice; peril because our society's structures are too often molded by the hands of a few.

A complete understanding of poverty is not one that comes with lavish living; instead, to stand in solidarity with the poor, we must don a certain element of poverty ourselves. In this partnership, we accompany each other on an even playing field where outcomes are shared, not by those who serve and those who are served, but by people together, striving for a more just world.

Questions for Reflection

St. Francis was careful to indicate to his brothers that he did not want them to receive things which were inconsistent with the way of poverty. Take a moment to think about his choice of poverty over lavish living. What might those reasons have been?

What would it mean for you to, as this author writes, stand in solidarity with the poor in big and small ways?

²⁵They shall not dare to seek any letter from the Roman Curia either personally or through an intermediary, neither for a church or for another place or under the guise of preaching or even for the persecution of their bodies.

Accepting Charity
Courtney (Murphy) Hull, Franciscan Volunteer Ministry

Our program was pretty strict compared to some others in the area (non-Franciscan, but still Catholic programs) and we sometimes felt like we were missing out. We had very strict rules about prayer, community nights and community dinners and although I am sure some communities did not follow every rule, we were very "by the book." For many of us, we were just learning about Francis but didn't know the intricacies of his Rule or what he instructed his brothers and sisters to do. We took our cues from the Franciscan men and women we worked with and also from Francis' commitment to living the Gospel just as Jesus did.

There were a few times we were treated to a nice dinner either with our benefactors or as "just a treat" paid for by benefactors. Although it felt awkward at the time, we also learned (from watching our Franciscan brothers and sisters) that there were people who really admired how we lived, and treating us to dinner or to Temple University basketball tickets was a way they could show their appreciation for us. As I said, it was awkward, but I learned that it is important to not just give charity but also to accept it at times.

Questions for Reflection

Francis warned his brothers to keep their commitment to poverty in mind when people offer them gifts. In what way does the writer do that?

Generosity entails not only giving but receiving things gracefully. Who has taught you to gracefully receive something?

²⁶*Wherever they have not been received, they shall flee into another land to do penance with the blessing of God.*

Rejection and Surrender
Katie Purple, Cap Corps, New York

I took a deep breath and began my testimony. I was standing before forty high school students, all of them total strangers, yet I was sharing with them a story of how God had captured my heart and helped me to better understand Him.

During my testimony, I kept a close eye on the sea of faces. Many looked like they were pondering what I said; perhaps my words reverberated in their own understanding of God. Others looked away and pretended not to be listening. I felt the pang of rejection and found it difficult not to take it personally.

I reminded myself, however, of why I was here in the first place. I was the sower in Matthew 13, simply planting seed. Some seed would never take root, but some seed would bury itself in rich soil and produce bountiful fruit. I would probably never see it; I could not follow up with the teenagers in following days to see how they had responded to my words. Instead, I could cling to the blind faith that Christ could water any seed which had been planted.

A moment of rejection was at the same time a moment of great surrender and great hope.

Questions for Reflection

Echoing Jesus' instructions to his followers in the Acts of the Apostles, St. Francis encourages his brothers to go from place to place preaching and spreading the Good News and to react to rejection by simply leaving the place and going someplace else. Describe a time when you felt that your efforts were not well received. Did you "flee into another land?"

Describe a moment when you felt, as the author describes, surrender and hope at the same time.

[27] ... I firmly want to obey the minister general of this fraternity and another guardian whom it might please him to give me. [28] And I want to be so captive in his hands that I cannot go anywhere or do anything beyond obedience and his will, for he is my lord.

Taking Criticism Well
David Carvalho, Cap Corps, New York

Just because you're passionate about your service doesn't mean you and your boss will always have the same perspective on things. As part of our work we created youth retreats. I was assigned to create a new workshop on "love" for high school students. After working on it for some time and bouncing it off several co-workers, I thought it was almost finished. However, a few days before the retreat, my boss took me aside and asked to talk to me about it. He had ideas to help the workshop function effectively. I have to say, I don't always take criticism well especially when I worked on this and took ownership of it. Regardless, I agreed to sit down with him. I explained my thinking, and he shared his concerns. We proceeded to brainstorm together, collaborating on the workshop in such a way that kept my original concept. Ultimately, it was better than what I had planned originally. Criticism will always come, even if it's hard to take. When it does, you might as well use it constructively.

Questions for Reflection

Toward the end of his life, when St. Francis wrote his Testament, he was no longer in charge of the fraternity of brothers. We see his humility and obedience here, as he says that he wants to be subject to another friar. In what ways have you struggled with obedience and authority?

What is the difference in the ways mature and immature people receive criticism? What is the relationship between criticism and obedience? What is the point of receiving criticism well?

[29]And although I may be simple and infirm, I want nonetheless always to have a cleric who will do the Office with me as it is contained in the Rule.

Recognition of God's Presence
Kathryn Kirkpatrick, Franciscan Volunteer Ministry

Before I began my year as a Franciscan volunteer, my prayer life was mundane and self-centered. I blessed my meals, and I prayed before I drifted to sleep at night. I prayed before taking college exams, and I asked God to guide me in my next journey after graduation. It was always ME talking, always ME asking God to help ME. Looking back, it seemed like a one-sided phone conversation. I must have been exhausting!

When I began my Franciscan Volunteer Ministry year, all the "stresses" of college were behind me. I was truly happy and I felt, for the first time, that I was actually where God had intended for me to be. I didn't feel the need to pray for myself, and although I was now attending Mass daily and surrounded by the most grounded and righteous people I've ever known, I realized my routine way of communicating with God was not working. I felt a little lost, like when you lose cell service or the line gets fuzzy. I would try to call back, but I just couldn't connect.

While in the midst of this prayer rut, we took our first Franciscan Volunteer Ministry retreat to Mt. Irenaeus Mountain Retreat, the most serene piece of wilderness I've ever encountered. I was convinced that at its altitude, it truly must be a place where Heaven and Earth meet. Between Mass, prayer, and activities, I searched my soul to find a secure connection with God again. During a morning prayer, He came to me in a stream of eight words: "Be still and know that I am God." I knew this verse, but I've never heard such blatant and profound instructions in my life. God spoke to me and I heard it. He said, "Hey, Kathryn, I'm here! Why don't you just hush and listen to me?!" From that moment on, my prayer life changed for the better. I now know that my silent recognition of God's presence is enough. I began to see God in the smiles and struggles of the Inn's guests; I heard Him in the street music of Kensington; and I felt His presence in my work and in the most unexpected of places and circumstances. Whenever prayer becomes hard for me now, nearly a year later, I simply sit back with no expectations and I listen.

Questions for Reflection

As St. Francis' life progressed, the nature of his prayer life changes as well. How has your prayer life changed over time?

Who is doing most of the talking in what this author calls your phone conversations with God?

[29]And although I may be simple and infirm, I want nonetheless always to have a cleric who will do the Office with me as it is contained in the Rule.

Praying through Obstacles
Kevin Cilano, Franciscan Volunteer Ministry

The kind of spirit drawn to the Franciscan Volunteer Ministry motto "love… lived in service" is particularly passionate.

Working for others is a challenge unto itself, but it is not service. Service is working with others, as equals, in loving, transformative empathy. Strangers become your sisters and brothers, and your work becomes intentionally, then naturally, lived.

It can also become very difficult to live with some of the human family and share in their pain and sorrows. At times, faith can be shaken and prayers, seemingly unanswered, weigh as a heavy burden. It might sound odd, but during such times when it's hard to pray…don't.

But don't give up, give it up.

Accept whatever is acting as an obstacle to your prayer. This is not giving in, some passive surrender while despairingly waving a white flag. This is actively recognizing and openly receiving turmoil and fears. Once you humbly embrace the situation, you can pray through the obstacle: give it up as a hopeful offertory prayer amidst a calming deep breath.

Then, passionately return to your community, ministry and prayer.

Questions for Reflection

St. Francis was sickly toward the end of his life. He acknowledges his sickliness and speaks out of humility when he says he wants to have a fellow friar with him who will make sure overcomes any obstacles to praying the Office. Name an obstacle to your prayer. How can you pray through this obstacle?

30 And all the other brothers shall be bound to obey their guardians and to do the Office according to the Rule.

Enriching my Prayer Life
Philip Lomneth, Franciscan Community Volunteers

During my year with a Franciscan volunteer program, for the first time I can remember, I let someone else accompany me deeply in my spiritual life. I had shared personal prayers with groups of people before, and I had gone on retreats and revealed parts of my spiritual life to people there. However, never before did I have a spiritual director with whom I met regularly over six months. During this year, however, someone was always there keeping me accountable and enriching my prayer life. Monthly, I would meet with my spiritual director and we would go over any significant events in my life, as well as my relationship with God. Whereas before I always took for granted my ability to analyze my prayer, my director opened new ways for me to think about and approach my relationship with God. Areas I passed over quickly, he encouraged me to dwell on and draw out the reasons why I wanted to skip over them. He asked me to explain when I would give vague answers to questions I didn't want to answer. He challenged some of my ideas about what it meant to be in relationship with God, which ultimately led to a richer understanding of how to pray.

Questions for Reflection

Why is prayer important?

The writer appreciated his spiritual director, who kept him accountable in prayer. Who does that for you?

Obedience isn't Easy
Lizzy Pugh, Cap Corps – East

Saint Francis said in his Testament that "the brothers shall be bound through obedience" to do the right thing (verse 31). At the beginning of my time in service, things weren't going well at my placement. I didn't know what my on-site supervisor expected, and consequently, I let her down regularly. I was serving inner city teenage mothers. I didn't know what to do, and thought that maybe I was wrong to follow my instincts into service. How could God expect me to love them? The girls cussed at me and were blatantly disrespectful. One student spat in my face. I wanted to back out- this wasn't what I thought it would be. My program supervisor encouraged me to persevere. She didn't say the word "obedience," but it was there beneath her words. If I believed God wanted me there, I needed to keep trying to see the students as God did. I needed to be obedient to what was right. By the year's end, I had bonded with my students. I was helping them prepare for the ACT while they taught me dance moves (I wasn't good.) I grew close to their children, rocking them to sleep and teaching them songs. I could have missed that if I did what I wanted, taking the easy way out. However, by being obedient, I was able to see my students and their children through God's eyes. Obedience isn't easy, but when we are obedient to what God wants for us, we can see things in a whole new light and learn what it means to follow Jesus.

Questions for Reflection

What would it take for you to go from having someone spit in your face to lovingly rock their children to sleep?

Describe a time that your obedience helped you see things in a whole new light.

[32]...*Guard him strongly as a prisoner day and night, so that he cannot be snatched from his hands until he can personally bring him into the hands of his minister.*

I Saw her Struggling
Krystle Morrison, Change a Heart Franciscan Volunteer Program

Bethany was the age of a first-grader, but she was in kindergarten. I met her at a homeless housing agency. She was frustrated; she was filling out worksheets with her peers and didn't have all the answers. I felt ill-equipped to help, but with several kids in the learning center, the after school instructor needed assistance keeping everyone engaged. I was assigned to work with the two kindergarteners. While her friend moved along independently, Bethany was still stuck on the first worksheet. She didn't know the names of all the colors. She could count, but didn't know how to write all the numbers. When I saw her struggling, I took a step back. We talked about our favorite things and interests – she had a lot of questions for me too – and avoided topics that damaged her confidence. I didn't want her to fall back into that negative place of frustration. By the time the after-school instructor was able to work with her, we had strayed far from the worksheets, but Bethany was smiling. I then watched and admired as the instructor brought educational components to the conversation and inspired her to want to learn, something I was not prepared to deal with.

Questions for Reflection

Describe a time when it was your job to care for someone until another more-qualified person was available to take over. What was the outcome?

Have you ever strayed from an assigned task in order to care for someone in need? How did you know that was the more important role to take?

In Hardship, Despair and Victory
Nick Despotidis, Cap Corps – East

From One Brother to Another:

"From one brother to another, I am happy for you Nick" were the words my best friend, Michael, said to me when he dropped me off at the volunteer house. We developed a brotherhood over four years, much like the brotherhood that would be sewn together by my volunteer community and service placement in the upcoming year. We were excited, not because something had ended but something new had begun.

In my community, we were five completely different people, from different parts of the country, with different reasons for coming. Despite these differences I knew it was going to work, simply because our intentions to help and love those in need had all been the same. My hypothesis was amazingly true, in times of hardship we persevered, in despair we wept, in victory we rejoiced, and in uncertainty we loved.

Today, I call my Capuchin Franciscan Volunteer community and those I served at the Spanish Catholic Center my family. When I recently was let go by my employer, I decided to return as a volunteer at the Center, and I was still welcomed with unswerving love. I was transformed by this experience and was baptized into the Roman Catholic Church a year later. I attribute who I am and who I will become to those I have met on my journey. We have developed friendships and created everlasting memories that will last until we see each other again.

Questions for Reflection

Describe a time when you were among others and, in times of hardship you persevered? Which victories did you rejoice with them?

38And I through obedience firmly command all my brothers, cleric and lay, not to place glosses on the Rule or on these words, saying: They are to be understood in this way.

What We Want to Do
Kirstin Elise van der Gracht, Volunteers in Mission

I don't like cursive. It takes a long time to write, and I really didn't want to have to teach it to a bunch of elementary school kids who have trouble with attention and phonological skills. Given the choice, I would have taught them print, but Sister Jenniffer asked me to teach cursive. I was volunteering with a friend as a special needs instructor in the Franciscan school in the barrio of Santo Domingo, where cursive is used much more than print. That was just one of many cultural obstacles I had to face. I was frustrated; I wanted to do things my way! But serving others doesn't mean pushing my values on them — it means doing what they ask of me (being obedient.) At first, I did as I was told, but only grudgingly. It was difficult to swallow my pride! Then, as the semester continued, the Lord opened my eyes. I learned that usually when Sister Jenniffer asked us to do something differently, it was because she knew what was best for her kids in their cultural context. Sometimes what we want to do is different than what God needs us to do, and His plan is always best.

Question for Reflection

Describe a time when you were frustrated because you wanted to do something your way then realized someone else's way was actually better.

[39]But as the Lord has given me to speak and to write the Rule and these words simply and purely, so shall you understand them simply and purely, without gloss, and observe them with holy activity until the end.

Understood Simply
Michael Lamanna, FrancisCorps

I cannot think of my experience of Franciscan simple living without thinking of my FrancisCorps community.

As a person who likes to use lots of stuff, my community challenged me to be conscious of how my lifestyle — from water use to travel time — affected them and others around me.

On the other hand, my community's openness to me being "me" allowed me to put what I had at the service of the community. One night in the Fall, I hosted a game night. I spent (relatively) a lot of money on random objects: lug-nuts, balloons, ping pong balls, kabob skewers... I wasn't sure about spending all of that money, but the material expense was outweighed by the joy of our communal time spent putting those objects to a very creative use through games.

When our gifts — material and otherwise — are put at the service of community, they become more than just things. God's will exists in all things — in our frugality and our feasting. Thomas Merton says, "Resting in God's glory above all pleasure and pain, joy or sorrow... we love in all things God's will rather than the things themselves, and that is the way we make creation a sacrifice in praise of God."

Questions for Reflection

What are some challenges of choosing frugality?

How can your choice to live simply affect others in your family, community, neighborhood or world?

40And whoever shall have observed these things, may he be filled in heaven with the blessing of the most high Father and on earth with the blessing of his beloved Son

Blessed with Belonging and Purpose
Emily Ford, Franciscan Outreach Volunteers

It was on a late night drive home when I realized that I was exactly where I belonged. I had lived in Chicago for a few weeks, but I had been so consumed by my work at the soup kitchen that I had little time to explore the area. After shadowing fellow community members' work at a homeless shelter, we took a detour up Lake Shore Drive, an expressway cushioned by Lake Michigan to the east and the Chicago skyline to the west. As I sat in the passenger seat, awed by God's beauty to my right and man's creation to my left, the weight of my service to our homeless guests lifted from me. In that place, which I continue to frequent in times of stress, I am reminded of how immense the world is, and that I belong in it. There's no better feeling than driving with my family of community members, turning up the music, and being overcome with a sense of belonging and purpose. Just like the beautiful and chaotic street we drive along, God has a path for us to follow too.

Questions for Reflection

St. Francis offers a heavenly and an earthly blessing to those who follow what he has described in his Testament. Is there a place you have found where it seems you catch a glimpse of God's creation and man's creation at the same time? Describe that place.

This writer describes a place which has provided her with peace and stress relief. Where do you go to find peace and stress relief?

[41]And I, little brother Francis, your servant, inasmuch as I can, confirm for you this most holy blessing both within and without.

Simply, Immensely Blessed
E. Ce Miller, Franciscan Common Venture

Half-way thorough a year of service in Los Angeles, I traveled to Honduras with the Franciscan Common Venture (FCV) program. My year of service in Los Angeles was not going well — I didn't feel like I was making a positive difference, and our community of volunteers was as fractured and broken as the gang-run neighborhood we lived in. When FCV sent out a call for short-term volunteers to help construct a pipeline for running water in Gracias, Honduras, I presented the idea to my community leader and immediately signed up.

Working alongside the community of Gracias, we volunteers spent our days digging trenches, and our evenings munching on cheesy tortillas and beans, and nursing sore muscles. The work in Honduras was physical — uncomplicated, but vital. It was tangible, visible work — throughout the day I could actually see what work I had accomplished. Our nights were filled with fellowship, storytelling and reflection. In just a short period of time, I found I'd made lifelong friendships. When I returned from Honduras, I felt renewed, reenergized, and hopeful.

"Gracias," as many know, means "thank you" in Spanish. It is also the perfect word to express how I feel about the community of Gracias, Honduras: thankful for the work, grateful for the community that welcomed me and simply, immensely blessed.

Questions for Reflection

Gratitude is at the core of living like Francis. For what do you have gratitude?

How have you been simply, immensely blessed?

*41And I, little brother Francis, your servant, inasmuch as I can,
confirm for you this most holy blessing both within and without.*

A Resonating Effect
Anna Lucas Marin, Franciscan Common Venture

Over three years ago, I arrived home from a 10-day trip to Honduras. In only a week and a half, my life changed. I witnessed tragedy and beauty, hardships and triumphs, people coming together and then being separated again. I witnessed the spoken language barrier, and even more, I realized the nonverbal language breakthrough. I witnessed strangers become dear friends and people, separated by borders, become family. I saw joy, love, and eloquence; all offset by nearby pain, sadness, and heartache.

Our team of twenty left with the mission of access to clean water, but we soon realized our mission encompassed much more. Our days were spent working alongside Hondurans in the villages of Cocina and Catulaca; our nights were celebrated in companionship with our team and our Honduran neighbors. Everywhere we voyaged, we were greeted with open arms and shown appreciation for our contribution. In collaboration with Catholic Relief Services, this project made clean water accessible to nearly 800 families, spanning seven rural villages.

The cooperation and organization of the Hondurans provided inspiration, and their courage in undertaking a project of this magnitude, fueled our work. Perhaps what was most humbling was witnessing those who seemingly have very little give abundantly.

Our neighbors left their doors open all night in case we needed to use the restroom, and community members prepared meals of their finest ingredients as a means to express their gratitude. We were shown generosity and selflessness, from the day we arrived, until the day we departed.

Most impactful, was my realization that it isn't what is given, but rather, how it is given. The people of Honduras taught me to treasure companionship. They exemplified the beauty of family; in fact, they exemplified beauty in every sense of the word. Looking back on this service, three years later, I am aware of the absolute blessing of these people, this experience, and the resonating effect it has had on me, even today.

Questions for Reflection

Francis blesses his brothers "within and without" — in what ways has God blessed you internally and externally?

Francis refers to himself as a little brother to others — when have you been welcomed and treated as a family member by others?

List of Franciscan Service Network Programs

The stories in this book were written by men and women who have volunteered through Franciscan Service Network programs. To find out how you can get involved, check out the website: www.franciscanservicenetwork.org.

Cap Corps – East
www.capcorps.capuchin.com
Cleveland, OH I Washington, DC I Papua New Guinea

Cap Corps – Midwest
www.capcorps.org
Detroit, MI I Chicago, IL I Milwaukee, WI I Nicaragua I Panama I Peru

Cap Corps – New York
http://www.capuchin.org/CapuchinYouthAndFamilyMinistry/ CapCorpsVolunteers
Garrison, NY

Change A Heart
www.changeaheartvolunteers.org
Pittsburgh, PA

Franciscan Community Volunteers
www.fcvonline.org
St. Cloud, MN

Franciscan Mission Service
www.franciscanmissionservice.org
Washington, DC I Latin America I Africa I the Caribbean

Franciscan Common Venture
www.osfdbq.org/venture_volunteer.php
Dubuque, IA

Franciscan Outreach Volunteers
www.franciscanoutreachvolunteers.org
Chicago, IL

Franciscan Volunteer Ministry
www.franciscanvolunteerministry.org
Camden, NJ | Philadelphia, PA |Silver Spring, MD

Franciscan Volunteers...No Risk, No Gain
www.osfphila.org/franciscanvolunteers
Greater Philadelphia, PA

FrancisCorps
www.franciscorps.org
Syracuse, NY | Costa Rica

Volunteers in Mission
www.bernardinevolunteers.org
Reading, PA | Dominican Republic

For more information on retreats and presentations on Saints Francis and Clare of Assisi, please visit:

Franciscan Passages
www.franciscanpassages.org